Govee WiFi Water Sensor 3 Pack User Guide

I0478172

A Practical Guide to Installation and App Mastery for Homeowner's with Tips & Tricks for Optimal Performance

Gabriel P.Jose

Table of Contents

Chapter 1

Introduction: Protecting Your Home with Smart Leak Detection

The High Cost of Water Damage

Imagine waking up one morning to the sound of water trickling. You look into it and find a leak in the pipe under your bathroom sink. The cabinet and the nearby drywall have been soaked by the accumulated water on the floor. What begins as a little annoyance soon turns into a big problem. You have to deal with damp carpets, crooked flooring, and the possibility of mold development. How much will repairs cost? Not to mention the stress and disturbance to your life, it might amount to thousands of dollars.

Unfortunately, this situation happens much too often. Every year, numerous homes are impacted by water damage, which is one of the main causes of property damage. Water has a cunning way of getting into troublesome areas, whether it's a busted pipe, a leaking appliance, or a malfunctioning fixture, causing damage to your house and your finances.

The cost of water damage might be quite high. The cost of replacing or repairing damaged insulation, flooring, and drywall may mount up rapidly. You may have structural damage that may need much more involved (and costly) repairs if the leak is ignored for a long time. Not to mention the possible health risks posed by mold, which may grow well in moist conditions and cause respiratory disorders as well as other health concerns.

However, the expenses are not only monetary. There are many ways that water damage may ruin your life. While repairs are being made, you may need to replace damaged items, cope with the annoyance of contractors and insurance adjusters, and move temporarily. As you deal with the stress of handling a leak's aftermath, the emotional toll may be substantial.

Fortunately, a large portion of this harm may be avoided. You may greatly lower the chance of serious water damage and safeguard both your house and your peace of mind by being proactive in identifying and fixing leaks as soon as they appear. Smart home technology may help you keep ahead of any leaks by providing creative solutions in this situation.

The Govee WiFi Water Sensor 3 Pack is one such option. This user-friendly and reasonably priced device monitors for leaks around the clock and notifies you right away if water is found. To ensure thorough coverage, you may strategically install its small sensors in areas such as basements, behind sinks, and next to appliances.
In addition to detecting leaks, the Govee Water Sensor instantly notifies your smartphone, enabling you to respond quickly whether you're at home or abroad. This quick action might be the difference between a little leak and a big catastrophe.

Despite being intended to be user-friendly, some customers have had difficulties with setup, WiFi connection, and app performance with the Govee Water Sensor. By giving you the information and resources you need to install and operate your Govee Water Sensor with confidence, this guide seeks to tackle those issues head-on and guarantee dependable leak detection and peak performance.

We'll go into the finer points of configuring your Govee Water Sensor, resolving typical problems, and becoming proficient with the Govee Home app in the next chapters. To make sure you're prepared to shield your house from the expensive and upsetting consequences of water damage, we'll also go over cutting-edge methods for maximizing sensor placement and sensitivity.

Introducing the Govee WiFi Water Sensor 3 Pack

Imagine this: you're away on vacation, loving the sun and sand, when a nagging fear creeps into your thoughts. Did I turn off the iron? Is the back door locked? And then, the big one: what if a pipe breaks while I'm gone? That mental picture of coming home to a wet basement, soaked rugs, and ruined furniture is enough to ruin anyone's trip.

Water damage is a homeowner's fear. It can strike suddenly, causing thousands of dollars in fixes, not to mention the stress and trouble of dealing with the fallout. But what if there was a way to catch leaks early, avoid major damage, and gain peace of mind, whether you're at home or miles away?

Enter the Govee WiFi Water Sensor 3 Pack – your watchful guardian against water leaks. This smart home device is meant to give you an early warning system, alerting you to the presence of water in sensitive parts of your house. Think of it as a network of tiny sentinels, standing guard in your basement, laundry room, or under the kitchen sink, ready to sound the alarm at the first sign of trouble.

Here's how it works: each pack comes with three small, battery-powered sensors and a center point. The sensors are put in places prone to leaks, and they constantly watch for the presence of water. When a sensor finds moisture, it causes an immediate warning, both on the sensor itself (a loud noise to alert anyone close) and through the Govee Home app on your smartphone.

The hub works as the brain of the system, connecting the devices to your home's WiFi network. This allows the devices to interact with your phone, giving quick messages wherever you are. So even if you're at work, on vacation, or simply in another room, you'll know right away if there's a possible leak.

Now, we know what you might be thinking. Setting up smart home gadgets can be scary, especially if you're not a tech whiz. But fear not! The Govee Water Sensor is built with user-friendliness in mind. While some users have reported issues with WiFi connection and app setup (we'll dig deeper into those in later chapters), the core functionality is simple.

The devices themselves are incredibly easy to use. Simply enter the batteries, place them in the chosen areas, and they're ready to go. The Govee Home app helps you through the setup process with step-by-step guidance and helpful images. Once everything is connected, you can watch your sensors, adjust alerts, and check battery life with just a few taps on your phone.

The Govee WiFi Water Sensor 3 Pack is more than just a leak monitor; it's your helper in home security. It gives you the power to avoid expensive water damage, protect your things, and enjoy peace of mind knowing that your home is always under watchful eyes, even when you're not there.

Benefits of Smart Leak Detection

The real advantages of intelligent leak detection go well beyond just avoiding expensive repairs, even if the effects of water damage are unquestionably dire. Let's examine in more detail how these clever gadgets might improve your life and provide priceless peace of mind.

Early Identification: The Secret to Reducing Damage
Conventional leak detection techniques often depend on visual examinations or, worse, identifying the issue after considerable harm has already been done. As watchful protectors, smart leak sensors such as the Govee WiFi Water Sensor provide 24-hour monitoring and prompt notifications at the first indication of an issue. To reduce the amount of water damage, early diagnosis is essential. You may avoid costly repairs, mold removal, and the possible loss of priceless belongings by promptly addressing a minor leak before it becomes a huge catastrophe.

Comfort: Safeguarding Your House Even When You're Not There
Consider this scenario: a pipe breaks in your basement while you are on vacation, enjoying a well-earned respite. You would arrive home to a flooded mess if you used conventional leak detection techniques. However, no matter where you are in the globe, the Govee WiFi Water Sensor will instantly notify you on your smartphone. This enables you to act right away and get in touch with a friend, neighbor, or plumber to resolve the problem before it becomes worse. Smart leak detection offers genuine peace of mind by allowing you to leave the house without having to worry about possible water damage all the time.

Preventative Action: Protecting Your Investment
In addition to being a substantial financial investment, your house serves as a haven and a location for creating memories. Proactively

safeguarding this investment is made possible by smart leak detection. Early detection and repair of leaks may help you avoid long-term damage that might compromise the structural soundness and value of your house. This proactive method protects your home's durability and integrity while also saving you money.

Benefits of Insurance: Possible Savings and Lower Risk

The importance of smart home technology in reducing risk is acknowledged by many insurance providers. Your homeowner's insurance rates may be reduced if you install a Govee WiFi Water Sensor. Certain insurers provide substantial discounts for preventative actions that lower the risk of claims. Additionally, you lower the possibility of future claims and any increases in your insurance premiums by demonstrating your dedication to leak prevention.

Easy Monitoring: A Smooth Transition to Your Smart Home

The Govee Home app and the Govee WiFi Water Sensor work together flawlessly to provide an intuitive interface for monitoring your sensors and getting notifications. For a fully connected experience, you can quickly check the status of each sensor, change the notification settings, and even link the sensors to other smart home appliances. You may keep informed without making your life more complicated thanks to this simple monitoring.

Environmental Responsibilities: Water Conservation and Earth Protection

Leaks add to needless waste, and water is a valuable resource. In addition to protecting your house, smart leak detection encourages environmental stewardship. You may save water and lessen your environmental impact by quickly finding and fixing leaks. Every drop matters in a world where water is becoming more scarce, and intelligent leak detection helps to protect this essential resource.

Beyond the Fundamentals: Improved Accessibility and Safety

Additional advantages provided by smart leak detection improve accessibility and safety for a range of people. The Govee WiFi Water Sensor adds an added degree of security for senior homeowners or those with limited mobility by warning them of leaks that they may not be able to readily see or access. This may provide a safer home environment by preventing slips and falls. Furthermore, homeowners who own rental properties or vacation homes may fix leaks quickly, even from a distance, thanks to the remote monitoring features, which provide priceless piece of mind.

A wise investment in the safety of your house, your financial security, and your peace of mind is smart leak detection. With the Govee WiFi Water Sensor 3 Pack, you can take charge, avoid expensive damage, and take advantage of all the advantages that come with having a fully smart home.

Chapter 2

Setting Up Your Govee Water Sensor: A Step-by-Step Guide

Downloading and Navigating the Govee Home App

Getting the Govee Home app is an essential first step in configuring your Govee WiFi Water Sensor. Your leak detection system's command center is this app, which lets you keep an eye on your sensors, get notifications, and change settings.

A smartphone or tablet with a steady internet connection is required to get started. Both iOS and Android smartphones may use the Govee

Home app.

For users of iOS devices (iPhone, iPad, and iPod Touch):
1. Launch the App Store: Find the App Store icon on the home screen of your smartphone. The symbol is blue with a white "A" enclosed in a circle.

2. Use the "Search" option at the bottom of the screen to look for the app. Type "Govee Home" into the search field and hit the "Search" key on your keyboard.

3. Find the app: The Govee Home app should be the first item that shows up in the search results. It has a stylized "G" in the middle of a white symbol.

4. Tap the "Get" button next to the app icon to download it. To verify the download, you may be asked to enter your Apple ID password or use Touch ID or Face ID.

5. Install the app: Your smartphone will automatically install the app when the download is finished. The app icon allows you to monitor your progress.

6. Launch the app: The Govee Home app will appear on your home screen upon installation. To open it, tap on the symbol.

Those who utilize Android devices (such as Samsung, Google Pixel, etc.):

1. Launch the Google Play Store by locating the icon on the home screen or app drawer of your smartphone. The triangle symbol has a lot of color.

2. Use the search box at the top of the screen to look for the app. On your keyboard, type "Govee Home" and hit the "Enter" key.

3. Locate the app: One of the top results ought to be the Govee Home app. It has a stylized "G" in the middle of a white symbol.

4. Tap the "Install" button next to the app icon to download it.

5. Install the app: Your smartphone will start to download and install the app. The progress may be seen in your notification bar or on the app icon.

6. Launch the application: The Govee Home app will appear on your home screen or in your app drawer when the installation is finished. To open it, tap on the symbol.

Troubleshooting Problems with Downloading
Here are some things to look for if you have trouble installing the app:

- Internet access: Make sure your device is connected to the internet reliably, using either mobile data or WiFi.
- capacity space: Verify that there is sufficient free capacity on your device to fit the app.
- Status of the Google Play Store and App Store: Periodically, there may be brief interruptions in the Google Play Store or App Store. If you think this could be the case, check their status online.
- Compatibility of devices: Although the majority of contemporary smartphones and tablets may run the Govee Home app, be sure your device satisfies the minimal operating system requirements.
- You may now go on to the following stage, which is to create a Govee account if the Govee Home software has been successfully loaded on your device. You can manage your devices, use the app's functions, and get crucial notifications about any leaks with this account.

Creating a Govee Account

You must first register for a Govee Home account before you can start using your Govee WiFi Water Sensor 3 Pack. Managing your sensors, getting alerts, and using all the Govee Home app's features are all done via this account. Let's go over each stage of the account creation process, answering any questions and making sure everything goes well.

Using the Govee Home Application

Your entryway to the world of intelligent leak detection is the Govee Home app. You must first download the app on your tablet or smartphone. Both iOS and Android smartphones may download the Govee Home app.

- For iOS users: Go to your device's App Store and look for "Govee Home." To download and install the app, tap the "Get" button.
- If you use an Android smartphone, go to the Google Play Store and look for "Govee Home." To download and install the app, tap the "Install" button.

After installing the app, find the Govee Home icon on the home screen of your smartphone and press to launch it.

Starting the Account Creation Process

A welcome screen will appear when you launch the Govee Home app for the first time. The features and advantages of the app are briefly summarized on this screen. Spend a minute becoming acquainted with the material that has been provided. Tap the "Sign Up" button at the bottom of the page to begin creating an account.

Giving Your Details

After that, the app will ask for your email address. Since this will be the main method of contact for alerts and account-related messages, make sure you have an active email address that you often check. Click "Continue" after your email address has been entered.

After that, a password creation prompt for your Govee Home account will appear. Select a secure password with a minimum of eight characters that consists of a mix of capital and lowercase letters, digits, and symbols. A strong password helps in preventing unwanted access to your account.

Verifying Your Email Address

Press the "Sign Up" button after entering your password and email address. To the email address you provide, Govee will send a verification email. Locate the Govee email by opening your inbox. The email may not arrive for a few minutes. Check your spam or trash folder if it's not in your inbox.

Click the "Verify Now" button or link in the verification email after opening it. Your Govee Home account will be activated and your email address verified as a result.

Finishing the Configuration

Once your email address has been validated, you will be sent back to the Govee Home app. Additional information, including your name and location, can be requested from you. This data guarantees that you get relevant alerts and notifications and helps customize your experience.

Fixing Issues with Account Creation

Even though creating an account is usually simple, there could be a few glitches along the way. To solve frequent problems, use these troubleshooting tips:

> ➤ The email address is invalid: Verify your email address one more time to make sure there are no typos or mistakes.
> ➤ Requirements for the password: Make sure your password satisfies the minimal criteria for both length and complexity. Use a password manager program to create and save safe passwords if you're having problems coming up with one.
> ➤ No email verification was received: Look for the email requesting verification in your spam or garbage folder. Try sending the verification email again from the Govee Home app if you're still unable to locate it.
> ➤ App bugs: Try shutting down and reopening the app or restarting your device if you run into any unforeseen difficulties or glitches while creating an account.

You are now prepared to start your path toward smart leak detection after creating your Govee Home account. To access a world of proactive home security, the next step is to connect your Govee WiFi Water Sensor gateway to your house's WiFi network.

Connecting the Gateway to WiFi (Troubleshooting Tips for Mesh Networks)

An illustrated manual for the Govee WiFi Water Sensor 3 Pack User Guide that explains how to connect the gateway to WiFi and offers troubleshooting advice for customers with mesh networks:
Setting up WiFi on the Gateway

1. Get the Govee Home App here:

❖ On your tablet or smartphone, open the Google Play Store or App Store.
❖ Look up "Govee Home" and download the app.
❖ If you have never used the app before, launch it and register.

2. Turn on the gateway by connecting the power adapter to a power outlet and plugging it into the gateway.

❖ The gateway's LED indication will illuminate.

3. To establish a WiFi connection, open the Govee Home app and press the "+" symbol located in the upper right corner.
Choose "Add Device" and then "Gateway."

❖ To connect the gateway to your WiFi network, adhere to the on-screen directions.

Important:

❖ Only 2.4 GHz WiFi networks are supported by the gateway. In order to connect the gateway to your mesh network, you may need to temporarily turn off your router's 5 GHz spectrum.
❖ Please follow the troubleshooting instructions below if you are experiencing issues connecting the gateway to your WiFi network.

4. Install the Water Sensors: o You may install the water sensors once the gateway is WiFi-connected.

❖ Tap the "+" symbol in the upper right corner of the Govee Home app.
❖ Choose "Add Device" and then "Water Sensor."
❖ To add each water sensor to the gateway, adhere to the on-screen directions.

Tips for Mesh Network Troubleshooting:

- You may need to temporarily turn off your router's 5 GHz spectrum if you are experiencing issues connecting the gateway to your mesh network.
- If you are still experiencing issues, please get in touch with Govee customer care.
- You may also try connecting the gateway to another WiFi network, such as a guest network.
- Extra Advice:
- Before connecting the gateway to your WiFi network, please disable any VPNs you may be using;
- Place the gateway in a central area with a strong WiFi signal;
- Keep the gateway away from other electronic devices that could disrupt the WiFi signal.

Tips for Resolving Issues

- Please use the following troubleshooting instructions if you are experiencing issues connecting the gateway to your WiFi network.
- For help, please get in touch with Govee customer service if you are still experiencing issues.
- Please consult the user manual or get help from Govee customer care if you are having any further problems with the Govee WiFi Water Sensor 3 Pack.

I hope this is useful!

Pairing the Sensors with the Gateway

Now that you've successfully gotten the Govee Home app and connected the router to your WiFi network, it's time to pair your Govee Water Sensors. This process is quick and easy, ensuring your sensors are easily blended into your smart home system.

1. Prepare the Sensors:
- Remove the battery pull tab from the bottom of each sensor.
- Locate the pairing button on the back of the sensor, typically marked by a small sign.

2. Open the Govee Home App:
- Launch the Govee Home app on your smartphone or computer.
- Ensure you're logged into your Govee account.

3. Add a Device:
- Tap the "+" button in the top right area of the app's main screen.
- Select "Water Sensor" from the list of possible devices.

4. Enter Pairing Mode:
- Follow the on-screen directions to enter pairing mode. This usually includes hitting and holding the pairing button on the sensor for a few seconds until the LED sign starts flashing quickly.

5. Select the Gateway:
- The app will instantly scan for open ports.
- Select the gateway you connected to your WiFi network earlier.

6. Confirm Pairing:
- The app will show a proof message once the sensor is properly paired.
- You can now give a custom name to your sensor for easy identification within the app.

7. Repeat for Additional Sensors:
- Follow the same steps above to pair each additional sensor in your Govee Water Sensor 3 Pack.

Visual Guide: For a more natural understanding, look to the related visual guide that shows the pairing process step-by-step. Each picture is clearly labeled and supported by concise directions, making it easy to follow along.

Additional Tips:
- If you find any problems during the pairing process, ensure that your smartphone or tablet is joined to the same WiFi network as the gateway.
- You can also try restarting the router or the Govee Home app to fix any connection problems.
- If the pairing process still fails, check the Govee user instructions or call Govee customer support for further help.

Remember:
- Pairing each sensor individually provides a smooth and successful link.
- Assigning custom names to your sensors helps you quickly identify and track them within the app.
- Refer to the graphic guide for a clear and thorough understanding of the matching process.

By following these simple steps and utilizing the provided visual guide, you'll have your Govee Water Sensors connected and ready to provide reliable leak detection for your home.

Testing the Sensors: Ensuring Accurate Leak Detection

Now that you've carefully followed the setup process and your Govee WiFi Water Sensors are properly placed throughout your home, it's time for the crucial final step: testing. This isn't just a routine; it's an important step to ensure your system is prepped and ready to identify leaks correctly, providing you with the peace of mind you deserve.

Why Testing Matters

Think of testing as a dress practice for your leak detection system. It's the chance to check that every component is working properly and speaking effectively. By modeling a leak, you can prove that:

- Sensors are Triggered: Ensure each sensor correctly detects the presence of water.
- Alarms Sound: Confirm that the built-in alarms on the sensors are loud enough to be heard.
- App Notifications Work: Verify that you receive quick alerts on your smartphone.
- Gateway Connectivity is Solid: Ensure the gateway is regularly sending data to the Govee Home app.

Testing offers faith that your system is ready to perform its vital job, keeping your home from possible water damage.

Step-by-Step Testing Guide

1. *Prepare Your Testing Area:* Choose a spot where you can safely test the sensors without causing any water harm. A sink, pool, or even a small bucket will work wonderfully.

2. *Gather Your Supplies:* You'll need a small amount of water and a dry cloth or paper towel to clean up afterward.

3. *Test Each Sensor Individually:* Start with the first sensor you paired with the gateway.

4. *Simulate a Leak:* Place the sensor straight into the water, ensuring the metal probes on the bottom are fully buried.

5. *Observe the Sensor's Response:* The sensor should quickly emit a loud sound. Note the loudness and intensity of the warning.

6. *Check for App Notifications:* Within seconds, you should receive a message on your smartphone through the Govee Home app. Observe the speed and clarity of the message.

7. *Repeat for Remaining Sensors:* Follow steps 3-6 for each of the remaining sensors in your Govee WiFi Water Sensor 3 Pack.

8. *Dry and Replace Sensors:* Once you've tried all the sensors, fully dry them with a cloth or paper towel. Return the monitors to their designated places in your home.

Fine-Tuning Your System
While studying, pay close attention to the following:
- Alarm Volume: Is the alarm loud enough to be heard throughout your home? If not, try moving the monitor or exploring ways to increase the sound.
- Notification Speed: How quickly did you receive the app notification? If there's a wait, examine possible WiFi connection problems.

- Sensor Sensitivity: Did the sensor start quickly upon touch with water? If not, look to Chapter 6 for tips on improving sensor sensitivity.

By carefully trying and fine-tuning your Govee WiFi Water Sensor system, you're taking proactive steps to safeguard your home from the devastating effects of water damage. This small investment of time can save you from major problems and costs in the long run.

Chapter 3

WiFi Connectivity Masterclass: Overcoming Common Challenges

Understanding 2.4 GHz vs. 5 GHz WiFi

The two primary frequencies in the world of WiFi are 2.4 GHz and 5 GHz. Imagine this as two distinct freeway lanes. Both will deliver you to your target, which is the internet! However, their speed and range are affected by distinct features.

WiFi at 2.4 GHz: The Long-Distance Passenger

This frequency is comparable to the highway's dependable, constant lane. Its signal may go further and more readily past obstructions like walls because of its larger range. Because of this, it's excellent for reaching devices that are distant from your router or for covering bigger households. It may be similar to traveling on a congested highway with a reduced speed limit, however, since it's a little older technology. This frequency is used by many devices, including outdated routers, Bluetooth devices, and microwaves, which may cause congestion and slower rates.

WiFi at 5 GHz: The Speed Demon

This frequency is comparable to a highway's fast lane. You can play online games, stream movies, and download things more quickly because of its higher bandwidth and quicker speeds. It's like being able to speed about on a broader, less crowded freeway. Its range is limited, however, as it finds it more difficult to get through obstructions like walls. Consider it a speed-oriented sports automobile that may not be the ideal option for negotiating an uneven, off-road path.

Which Govee Water Sensor Frequency Is Best for You?

The crucial component is that the gateway, which is what links the Govee WiFi Water Sensor to your WiFi network, is designed to operate only on the 2.4 GHz band. This is due to the fact that it puts a dependable connection ahead of the quickest speeds. Keep in mind that even if the sensors are behind appliances or in a basement, they must remain linked to your WiFi network in order to provide you with those vital leak notifications.

Troubleshooting Tip: Turning off your router's 5 GHz band for a while will frequently assist if you're experiencing issues connecting your Govee gateway to your WiFi network. This guarantees that the gateway and your smartphone are using the same 2.4 GHz frequency, which facilitates a more seamless connection. You may often re-enable the 5 GHz spectrum for your other devices when the gateway is connected.

You can resolve connection issues and make sure your Govee WiFi Water Sensor is constantly online and prepared to safeguard your network by being aware of the subtleties of these WiFi frequencies. home.

Troubleshooting Connection Issues

Even the most tech-savvy homeowner may sometimes have WiFi connection issues, despite the Govee WiFi Water Sensor's user-friendly setup. Do not be alarmed! This chapter gives you a thorough troubleshooting toolkit to overcome such obstacles and guarantee that your leak detection system is consistently connected.

Before Starting: The Fundamentals

Let's review some basic ideas that often fix the most prevalent connection problems:

- Power Cycle Everything: Start by rebooting your smartphone, Govee Gateway, and WiFi router. This little action may often fix short-term issues and restart network connections.
- Location, Location, Location: Make sure the Govee Gateway is placed in the middle of your house, as close as possible to the sensors and your WiFi network. The gateway should not be positioned close to walls, big appliances, or other electronics that can disrupt the WiFi signal.
- Accuracy of Password: Verify again that the WiFi password you supplied during setup is accurate. The gateway may not connect if one character is entered incorrectly.

Fixing Particular Situations

Let's now discuss some particular situations that were brought up in the user reviews:

- The 5 GHz Dilemma: The Govee Gateway uses the 2.4 GHz WiFi band, as we previously covered. During setup, make sure your smartphone is linked to the 2.4 GHz network if your router broadcasts both 2.4 GHz and 5 GHz networks. To prevent misunderstanding, momentarily turn off your router's 5 GHz network if needed.

Mysteries of Mesh Networks: Despite having great coverage, mesh WiFi networks may sometimes pose special difficulties. Try the following actions if you're utilizing a mesh network (such as Eero, as indicated in the reviews):

> Turn Off Band Steering: During setup, consider turning off any "band steering" features that your mesh system may have that swap device between frequencies automatically.

> Make Your Network Name and Password Simpler: The Govee Gateway may not operate with certain mesh systems' complicated network names or passwords. Consider setting up a guest network with a more straightforward name and password.

> Get in touch with Govee Support: If you're still having trouble, their staff may be able to provide tailored guidance for your mesh network model.

> The Vanishing Gateway Case: Try these actions if the Govee Gateway shows as offline in the app:

> Examine the LED on the gateway: A successful WiFi connection is shown by a solid blue light. For troubleshooting instructions, see the gateway's user manual if the light is off or blinking.

> Clear the Gateway: To return the gateway to factory settings, press and hold the reset button (find the button in the user manual). The setup procedure should then be repeated.

> Check for Router Updates: Make sure the firmware on your WiFi router is current. Compatibility problems may sometimes be caused by outdated firmware.

The Puzzle of "Govee_Gateway_XXXX": To get started, the software tells you to join a WiFi network called "Govee_Gateway_XXXX." If this network is not shown in your WiFi settings:

Make sure the pairing mode is selected on the gateway. The LED on the gateway should be flashing blue slowly. Otherwise, hold down the WiFi pairing button until pairing mode is activated.

Verify WiFi Visibility: Certain WiFi networks may be hidden by settings on certain cellphones. Make sure that this option is turned off.
Bring Yourself Nearer to the Gateway: The range of the "Govee_Gateway_XXXX" network is constrained. In this stage, move your smartphone closer to the gateway.

Anomalies Related to Apps: If alerts aren't coming in or the Govee Home app isn't showing the right sensor status:
- ➤ Power Shut off the application: Close the Govee Home app completely, then open it again. This often fixes little bugs.
- ➤ Verify the app's permissions to make sure it has everything it needs to deliver alerts and connect to WiFi.
- ➤ Reinstall the App: Try removing and reinstalling the Govee Home app if all previous attempts have failed. This often fixes more enduring problems.

Advanced Troubleshooting
Try these more sophisticated methods if you've tried all the fundamental troubleshooting stages and the connection problem persists:
- ★ Static IP Address: In the router's settings, give the Govee Gateway a static IP address. Stability may sometimes be enhanced by this.
- ★ WiFi Channel Optimization: To find less crowded WiFi channels, use a WiFi analyzer app. Switch to a less crowded WiFi channel on your router.
- ★ Firewall and Security Settings: Turn off any firewalls or router advanced security settings that could be preventing the Govee Gateway from connecting for the time being.

Looking for Professional Help
Do not hesitate to get in touch with Govee's customer service staff if you have attempted every troubleshooting step and are still having

issues. They may provide individualized support and have access to more comprehensive technical expertise.

Keep in mind that problems with WiFi access may often be resolved with a little perseverance and patience. You can make sure your Govee WiFi Water Sensor stays dependable and gives you the peace of mind you deserve by using the tools and troubleshooting techniques listed below.

Simplifying Your WiFi Password

In the age of smart home technologies, where convenience and connection are paramount, it's easy to forget the critical component of network security. As mentioned in several user reviews, the Govee WiFi Water Sensor, like many other smart gadgets, may need changes to your WiFi password during setup. While this may create worries about your network's security, do not worry! We'll walk you through the process of simplifying your password while maintaining your digital security.

Understanding the Need for Simplicity.
Why do certain smart gadgets, such as the Govee Water Sensor, struggle with complicated WiFi passwords? The solution lies in their embedded systems and limited computing power. These devices are intended to perform certain jobs, such as detecting breaches and delivering alarms, rather than decoding long, sophisticated passwords.

Consider this: you would not expect a simple calculator to tackle complicated equations designed for a supercomputer. Similarly, certain smart gadgets demand a simpler solution to WiFi authentication.
Striking the right balance of Security and Simplicity

The good news is that you may simplify your WiFi password without making your network susceptible to unauthorized access. Here's how.

1. Evaluate Your Password: If your existing password is a jumble of characters, consider generating a unique password for your smart home devices. This removes your most important personal accounts (email, banking, etc.) from your smart home network.

2. Select a Strong but Manageable Password: Aim for a password of at least 12 characters with a mix of capital and lowercase letters, digits, and symbols. Avoid utilizing popular terminology and personal information.

3. Consider a passphrase: A passphrase is a string of words that creates a memorable password. For example, "WaterSensorProtectsMyHome!" is a powerful and memorable phrase.

4. Use Password management: Password management may help handle several passwords efficiently. These programs create and store secure passwords, making your digital life easier while ensuring security.

5. Enable WiFi network encryption with WPA2 or WPA3, the most secure methods available. This provides a strong layer of security, even with a somewhat simpler password.

6. Update Router Firmware: Manufacturers often issue firmware upgrades to address security vulnerabilities. Keeping your router up to date is critical for ensuring a secure network.

7. Monitor Network Activity: Keep track of devices connecting to your WiFi network. If you see anything unusual, investigate and take proper action.

Additional Security Measures.

While simplifying your WiFi password for smart home devices is often required, you may further increase your network security by:

- Establishing a Guest Network: Provide a secondary WiFi network for guests to protect your core network from possible dangers.
- Enable a firewall: A firewall serves as a protective barrier between your network and the outside world, preventing illegal access attempts.
- Using VPN: A Virtual Private Network (VPN) encrypts your internet traffic, providing an additional degree of protection, particularly while utilizing public WiFi.

Security is an ongoing process.

Remember that network security is a continuous effort rather than a one-time job. Maintain up-to-date knowledge of the most recent security risks and best practices, and assess and upgrade your security measures as needed. By being proactive and knowledgeable, you may enjoy the benefits of smart home technology without jeopardizing your digital security.

Using an Older Device for Initial Setup

While the Govee WiFi Water Sensor is intended for easy setup, user evaluations have shown that connecting the gateway to your home's WiFi network might sometimes bring unanticipated issues. If you've had trouble with this procedure, an unexpectedly effective answer might be hidden in your drawer: an old smartphone or tablet. Let's look at why this out-of-date technology might be useful when setting up your Govee Water Sensor.

The 2.4GHz Advantage

Modern routers often operate on two WiFi frequency bands: 2.4 GHz and 5 GHz. While 5 GHz speeds are quicker, they have a lower range and may struggle to penetrate walls and other obstructions. Older devices, especially those made before the widespread use of 5 GHz WiFi, usually only support the 2.4 GHz band. This constraint might potentially be beneficial when configuring your Govee Water Sensor.

The Govee gateway is meant to operate on the 2.4 GHz band, which provides a longer range and better penetration through walls. By utilizing an older device that only supports 2.4 GHz, you may avoid possible conflicts and simplify the connecting procedure. This is especially useful if you have a large home network with many devices vying for bandwidth on the 5 GHz frequency.

Simplifying the setup process.

Using an older gadget for the first setup may simplify the procedure and lessen the risk of mistakes. Here's why.

- Reduced interference: With fewer devices vying for bandwidth on the 2.4 GHz band, your older device's connection to the Govee gateway is likely to be stronger and more consistent.
- Older devices have simpler WiFi settings, reducing confusion and conflicts compared to newer devices with sophisticated configurations.
- Improved compatibility: The Govee gateway may work better with older WiFi chipsets, resulting in smoother connections.

Step-by-Step Guide for Using an Older Device

1. Charge Your Older Device: Make sure your smartphone or tablet has enough juice to finish the setup procedure.

2. Download the Govee Home App. Install the Govee Home app on your previous device.

3. Follow the in-app instructions. Use the older device to connect the gateway to your WiFi network by following the in-app instructions.

4. join the Gateway's WiFi: During setup, your device will be requested to join the temporary WiFi network. This is an important step for setting the gateway's connection to your home WiFi.

5. Complete Setup: Connect the gateway to your home WiFi and couple the sensors.

6. Switch back to your primary device. Once the initial setup is complete, you may resume monitoring and managing your Govee Water Sensors using your main smartphone or tablet.

Important Considerations:

- Device compatibility: Ensure that your older device matches the minimal requirements for the Govee Home app. For compatibility information, refer to the app's description on the App Store.
- Check whether your older gadget can connect to your home's 2.4GHz WiFi network.
- Regularly update the Govee Home app on older devices for maximum functionality.

Beyond Initial Setup

While an older device may be useful for initial setup, keep in mind that you will most likely want to use your main smartphone or tablet for continuing monitoring and administration of your Govee Water Sensors. This enables you to fully use the app's features, such as getting real-time alerts, adjusting settings, and connecting with other smart home devices.

By exploiting the simplicity and focused connection of an older device, you may avoid possible WiFi issues and guarantee a simple setup procedure for your Govee WiFi Water Sensor. This innovative strategy may save you time and effort, enabling you to immediately enjoy the peace of mind that comes with smart leak detection.

Chapter 4

Mastering the Govee Home App: Unlocking its Full Potential

Navigating the App Interface

The Govee Home app is your central hub for monitoring and managing your Govee WiFi Water Sensor 3 Pack. This user-friendly app provides a clear and intuitive interface, allowing you to easily access all the information and settings you need to ensure your home is protected from leaks. Let's delve into the key sections of the app and explore their functionalities:

1. Home Screen:

- ❖ Sensor Status: This section displays the real-time status of each sensor in your network. You'll see icons indicating whether each sensor is online, offline, or has detected a leak.
- ❖ Battery Life: View the remaining battery life for each sensor, allowing you to proactively replace batteries before they run out.
- ❖ Alerts: This section displays a history of all sensor alerts, including the time, date, and type of alert triggered.
- ❖ Quick Access Buttons: Conveniently access essential functions like adding new devices, silencing alarms, and configuring settings.

2. Device Details:

→ Tapping on a sensor in the Home Screen takes you to its dedicated Device Details page.

→ Sensor Name: Edit the name of the sensor for easy identification and organization.

→ Location: View the sensor's location within your home.

→ Battery Life: Monitor the remaining battery life and set up low-battery notifications.

→ Sensor History: View a detailed history of the sensor's activity, including leak detections, alarms triggered, and battery level changes.

→ Settings: Customize the sensor's sensitivity level, configure notification settings, and enable/disable automatic shutoff for connected smart devices.

3. Automation:

- Create automated rules to trigger actions based on sensor activity.
- For example: Set up a rule to automatically turn off your water supply if a leak is detected.
- Integrate with other smart home devices to create a comprehensive leak protection system.

4. Settings:

➤ Manage your Govee Home account settings.

➤ Configure app notifications and preferences.

➤ Connect the app to other smart home platforms.

➤ Access FAQs and troubleshooting guides.

5. More:

➤ Discover additional Govee smart home products.

➤ Access community forums and support resources.

➤ Provide feedback and suggestions to the Govee team.

Visual Guide:

To complement the textual descriptions, here's a visual guide to the Govee Home app interface:

By familiarizing yourself with the layout and functionalities of the Govee Home app, you can unlock its full potential and effectively manage your Govee WiFi Water Sensor 3 Pack. Remember, the app is your essential tool for staying informed, taking proactive measures, and enjoying the peace of mind that comes with knowing your home is protected from water damage.

Understanding Sensor Status and Alerts

The Govee Home app serves as a command center for monitoring and controlling your WiFi Water Sensors. Understanding how to understand the information it produces is critical for using the system efficiently and keeping your house safe from water leaks. Let's look at the important features of the app UI and how to interpret the status updates and notifications it offers.

Sensor Status Icons: A Visual Guide.
When you launch the Govee Home app, you will be presented with a list of your connected sensors. Each sensor is represented by an icon, which gives a rapid visual indicator of its current state. Here is a rundown of the most frequent status symbols you'll encounter:

- The Blue Water Drop shows that the sensor is operational and has not detected any water.
- The red water drop with an exclamation mark indicates that the sensor has detected water and is generating an alert. This demands rapid care.

37

- The grey water drop indicates that the sensor is presently offline or having a connectivity difficulty. You may need to troubleshoot the sensor or monitor its battery life.
- Battery icon: The battery indication appears next to each sensor symbol. A full battery indicator shows a healthy battery, but a low battery icon alerts you that the battery has to be replaced soon.

Alert Notifications: Staying Informed

The Govee Home app sends you real-time notifications of any identified leaks or changes in sensor status. These warnings may be sent in a variety of ways, including:
- Push Notifications: Receive instant notifications on your smartphone screen, even while the app is closed.
- Email Notifications: Receive detailed notifications with a record of the occurrence.
- In-App Notifications: Alerts inside the Govee Home app provide more context and action choices.

Interpreting Alert Messages

When a sensor detects water, you will get an alert message including detailed details about the occurrence. Here's what you should look for:
- ★ Sensor Name: The alert will specify which sensor was activated.
- ★ The leak's precise time of detection is recorded.
- ★ If you identify your sensors with particular locations (e.g., "Basement Laundry Room"), the alert will contain that information.

Additional details:

Some alarms may provide additional information, such as the length of the leak or the sensor's current battery level.

Troubleshooting Sensor Status.

If you discover a sensor state that signals a problem (for example, offline or low battery), the Govee Home app includes troubleshooting options. You may get extensive information about each sensor, which includes:

➢ Last Connection Time: Indicates when the sensor last interacted with the gateway.
➢ Signal Strength: Measures the wireless connection between the sensor and gateway.
➢ Battery Level: Shows remaining battery life with greater accuracy.

Customizing Alert Settings

The Govee Home app enables you to tailor your alert settings to your interests and lifestyle. You may choose your preferred notification channels, such as push notifications, email, or in-app.

- Control alert frequency for ongoing leaks.
- Set Quiet Hours to avoid notifications during certain hours, such as nighttime.
- Customize alert sounds for various occasions.

By learning the Govee house app and its many warnings and status indications, you can proactively monitor your house for leaks and take immediate action to avoid damage. The app allows you to keep informed and in control, ensuring that your Govee WiFi Water Sensor 3 Pack delivers the best protection for your house.

Customizing Notification Settings

The Govee Home app is your command center for managing your WiFi Water Sensors, providing a wealth of information and control at your fingertips. One of its most powerful features is the ability to customize notification settings, ensuring you receive alerts in a way that aligns perfectly with your preferences and lifestyle. Let's explore how to fine-tune these settings to maximize your peace of mind.

Understanding Notification Options

The Govee Home app offers two primary notification methods:
- Push Notifications: These are instant alerts delivered directly to your smartphone or tablet through the Govee Home app. They appear as pop-up messages on your device's screen, even when the app is closed, ensuring you're immediately informed of a potential leak.
- Email Notifications: These alerts are sent to the email address associated with your Govee account. While not as immediate as push notifications, they provide a reliable backup notification method, especially if you might miss a push notification or have your phone on silent mode.

Customizing Notification Settings

1. Access Notification Settings: Open the Govee Home app and tap on the "Profile" icon in the bottom right corner of the screen. Then, select "Notification Settings."

2. Enable/Disable Notifications: You'll find separate toggles for enabling or disabling push notifications and email notifications. Choose the notification methods that best suit your needs.

3. Customize Push Notifications: If you enable push notifications, you can further customize their behavior:

➢ Show Previews: Choose whether to display a preview of the notification content on your lock screen. This can be helpful for quickly assessing the situation, but you may prefer to disable previews for privacy reasons.

➢ Sound: Select a notification sound from your device's library or choose to have no sound at all. Consider a distinct sound that will grab your attention in case of a leak.

➢ Vibration: Enable or disable vibration alerts for push notifications. This can be helpful if you keep your phone on silent mode but still want to be physically alerted to a potential leak.

4. Customize Email Notifications: If you enable email notifications, you can adjust the following:

☐ Frequency: Choose how often you want to receive email notifications. Options may include "Immediately," "Hourly Digest," or "Daily Digest." Consider your typical response time and how frequently you want to be updated.

☐ Content: Customize the information included in email notifications. You may be able to choose which events trigger an email (e.g., water detected, low battery, sensor offline).

5. Sensor-Specific Notifications: For more granular control, you can customize notification settings for each individual sensor. This allows you to tailor alerts based on the sensor's location and the potential severity of a leak in that area. For example, you might choose to receive both push and email notifications for a sensor placed near your washing machine, while only enabling push notifications for a sensor in a less critical area.

Fine-Tuning for Your Lifestyle

Consider your daily routine and how you typically use your smartphone when adjusting notification settings. If you tend to keep your phone on silent mode or often miss push notifications, enabling email notifications as a backup can provide an extra layer of assurance. Conversely, if you rely heavily on your phone and prefer instant alerts, prioritize push notifications with a distinct sound and vibration pattern.

Testing Your Customized Settings

After customizing your notification settings, it's crucial to test them thoroughly. Simulate a leak with each sensor and observe how the notifications behave. Verify that you receive alerts promptly and in the manner you expect. This ensures your system is configured to provide timely warnings and maximize your peace of mind.

Beyond the Basics

The Govee Home app may offer additional notification features, such as:

- Do Not Disturb: Schedule periods when you don't want to receive notifications, such as overnight.
- Notification History: Review a log of past notifications to identify any trends or potential issues.
- Third-Party Integrations: Explore integrations with other smart home platforms or notification services for even more customized alerts.

By mastering the Govee Home app's notification settings, you transform your Water Sensors into a truly personalized leak detection system, tailored to your specific needs and preferences. This empowers you to stay informed and take swift action, protecting your home from potential water damage while enjoying unparalleled peace of mind.

Monitoring Battery Life (and Addressing Inaccuracies)

The Govee Home app is your command center for monitoring your WiFi Water Sensors, delivering useful information about their state and performance. Battery life is an important consideration. While the Govee WiFi Water Sensor has a long battery life, it must be monitored carefully to guarantee continuous leak detection and prevent unexpected shocks. Let's look at how to utilize the app's battery monitoring tools and address some of the issues highlighted by users.

Understanding Battery Life Indicators.

The Govee Home app visualizes the battery life of each sensor. Typically, you'll notice a battery symbol with a percentage indication or a sequence of bars that fade as the battery drains. A full battery is shown by 100% or a complete set of bars, while a depleted battery is represented by a much lower percentage or fewer bars.

Addressing Potential Inaccuracies.

Some users have observed periodic errors in the app's battery life readings. This might be due to a variety of reasons, including brief communication problems between the sensor and the gateway or delays in the app updating the information. While Govee is always trying to enhance the app's accuracy, there are several proactive actions you may take:

- Refresh the app. If you feel a battery reading is incorrect, try refreshing the app by swiping it down on the screen. This compels the program to get the most recent data from the sensors.
- Restart the gateway. Sometimes restarting the gateway might assist address communication difficulties and guarantee proper data flow.
- Check sensor connectivity. Ensure that the sensors are within range of the gateway and have not been mistakenly relocated or blocked.
- Proactively replace batteries every 6-12 months, even if the app shows a modest battery level. This helps to prevent unexpected interruptions in leak detection.

Tips for Effective Battery Monitoring.

- Check the battery status of your sensors in the Govee Home app at least once per month. This enables you to detect any possible concerns early on.
- Check notification settings to allow low-battery notifications. This will serve as a timely reminder to replace the batteries before they entirely drain.
- High-quality alkaline batteries provide excellent performance and lifespan. Avoid using rechargeable batteries as they may not deliver constant voltage and compromise sensor accuracy. • When installing batteries, ensure they are placed properly and match the polarity specified in the battery compartment.
- Avoid installing sensors in harsh temperatures as they might impact battery life.

Beyond Battery Monitoring

While battery life is a crucial factor to consider, keep in mind that the Govee Home app has a slew of other useful functions. Spend some time exploring the app's settings and functions, such as:

- Customize Alert alerts: Receive alerts by email, push, or both.
- Adjust sound Volume: Ensure the sensor's sound is heard throughout your house.
- Rename sensors with descriptive names (e.g., "Basement Sensor," "Kitchen Sink") for easier identification.
- Organize monitoring by grouping sensors based on location or function.
- Investigate the app's automation options to link water sensors with other smart home devices for more control and convenience.

By understanding the Govee house app and its battery monitoring features, you can keep your WiFi Water Sensors ready to detect leaks and safeguard your house. This proactive strategy, along with the app's other useful features, allows you to take charge of your home's safety while reaping the numerous advantages of smart leak detection.

Chapter 5

Sensor Placement Strategies: Maximizing Leak Detection

Identifying High-Risk Areas in Your Home

Common Leak-Prone Areas:

1. Under Sinks: This is a common area for leaks due to loose connections, worn-out washers, and corroded pipes.

2. Behind Appliances: Leaks can occur behind washing machines, dishwashers, and refrigerators due to faulty hoses, loose connections, and drain pan overflows.

3. Around Toilets: Leaks can develop from the toilet tank, flapper valve, or supply line.

4. Near Bathtubs and Showers: Leaks can occur from the showerhead, faucet, or drainpipe.

5. In the Basement: Leaks can occur from sump pumps, water heaters, and washing machines.

6. In the Attic: Leaks can occur from roof leaks, HVAC systems, and condensation.

- Pay attention to any water stains on walls, ceilings, or floors.
- Listen for any dripping or running water sounds.
- Check your water meter regularly for any sudden increases in water usage.
- Have your plumbing system inspected by a professional every few years.

Optimal Placement for Each Sensor

While the Govee WiFi Water Sensor 3 Pack delivers dependable leak detection, its usefulness is enhanced when the sensors are properly distributed around your house. Consider these sensors your first line of defense against water damage, and their location is critical to their capacity to detect breaches quickly and correctly. Let's look at the best placement options for each sensor, taking into consideration the distinctive layout and probable leak-prone regions in various dwellings.

Sensor 1: The Kitchen Sink Sentinel.

The kitchen is often regarded as the heart of the house, but it is also a great site for possible water leaks. Dishwashers, trash disposals, and the sink, with its network of pipes and connections, are all potential hazards. To protect this busy hub, position your first sensor strategically under the kitchen sink.

Position the sensor adjacent to the water supply lines and drainpipe, with the probes pointing downward. This enables immediate identification of any drips or leaks from the sink's piping or appliances.

For further protection, place a tiny absorbent pad or piece of cardboard behind the sensor to increase its sensitivity to little spills.

Sensor 2: Guardian of the Water Heater.

Water heaters, although necessary for contemporary comfort, are known for leaking over time. A faulty water heater may spill gallons of water, causing extensive damage to your property. Therefore, allocating your second sensor to this appliance is a sensible investment.

Place the sensor on the floor precisely under the water heater, making sure it is not blocked by any items. If your water heater is in a restricted location, such as a closet or utility room, place the sensor just outside the door to guarantee the alert sounds. Inspect the water heater on a regular basis for symptoms of corrosion or leaks, and if any problems arise, contact a certified plumber.

Sensor 3: Bathroom Vigilance

Bathrooms, with their many water sources, are another high-risk location for leaks. Toilets, sinks, and showers all have potential weaknesses. For maximum protection, position your third sensor in the bathroom's most leak-prone region.

If you have a history of toilet leaks or are concerned about the wax ring seal, place the sensor behind the toilet and close to the base. This enables prompt identification of any leaks that may occur from the toilet's connection to the floor. If you're concerned about the sink or shower, position the sensor under the vanity or near the shower drain, with the probes pointing downwards.

Adapting to Your Home's Unique Layout

While these placement guidelines serve as a broad guideline, they must be tailored to your home's individual layout and possible risks. Consider the following.

- Older appliances are more likely to leak. Prioritize sensor installation near aged dishwashers, washing machines, and refrigerators with icemakers.
- Prioritize sensor installation based on plumbing history to prevent leaks in certain regions.
- Consider installing a sensor to monitor your home's basement or crawl space, which are commonly missed.
- Consider installing additional sensors to monitor exterior faucets and hose connections, particularly during cold weather.

Maximizing sensor effectiveness.

Beyond smart positioning, here are some more methods to ensure your sensors are constantly ready to detect leaks:

- Ensure sensors are not obscured by furniture, carpets, or other anything that may interfere with water detection.
- Ensure clear line of sight between sensors and gateway for effective signal transfer.
- Regularly test your sensors by simulating a leak to ensure proper functionality and communication with the app.
- Monitor battery life in Govee Home app to prevent disturbances in leak detection. Replace batteries soon.

By strategically installing your Govee WiFi Water Sensors and according to these best practices, you can establish a complete leak detection system that gives ongoing safety and precious peace of mind.

Avoiding False Alarms

The Govee WiFi Water Sensor is your steadfast ally in the fight against water damage, but even the most reliable systems can occasionally throw a curveball in the form of a false alarm. While these instances are generally rare, understanding the common causes and implementing preventive measures can minimize unnecessary disruptions and ensure your system operates with optimal accuracy.

Identifying the Culprits Behind False Alarms

False alarms can stem from various sources, often related to the sensor's environment or placement. Some common culprits include:

- Splashing Water: If a sensor is placed in an area prone to splashing water, such as near a shower or sink, droplets may inadvertently trigger the alarm.
- High Humidity: Excessive humidity or condensation can sometimes accumulate on the sensor's probes, leading to a false detection.
- Cleaning Products: Certain cleaning solutions, especially those with high conductivity, can trigger the sensor if they come into contact with the probes.
- Electrical Interference: In rare cases, electrical interference from nearby appliances or devices can disrupt the sensor's functionality and cause false alarms.
- Sensor Malfunction: While uncommon, a faulty sensor may occasionally trigger false alarms.

Strategies to Minimize False Alarms

- By implementing a few proactive measures, you can significantly reduce the likelihood of false alarms and ensure your Govee WiFi Water Sensor operates with precision:

- Strategic Placement: Carefully consider the location of each sensor, avoiding areas prone to splashing water or excessive humidity. For example, under a sink, place the sensor towards the back of the cabinet, away from potential drips or spills.

- Protective Barriers: If a sensor must be placed in an area where splashing is unavoidable, consider using a small protective barrier, such as a plastic cover or a strategically placed piece of waterproof tape, to shield the probes from direct contact with water droplets.

- Mindful Cleaning: When cleaning around the sensors, avoid using highly conductive cleaning solutions or spraying liquids directly on the devices. Instead, opt for a damp cloth or a gentle cleaning wipe.

- Humidity Control: If humidity is a concern, consider using a dehumidifier in the area where the sensor is located. This can help prevent condensation from forming on the sensor's probes.

- Regular Inspections: Periodically inspect your sensors to ensure they are clean, dry, and free from any obstructions that could interfere with their functionality.

- Sensor Testing: Regularly test your sensors by simulating a leak to confirm they are working correctly. This can help identify any potential malfunctions early on.

Troubleshooting Persistent False Alarms

- If you experience persistent false alarms despite implementing preventive measures, further investigation may be necessary. Consider the following:
- Relocate the Sensor: If a sensor consistently triggers false alarms in a particular location, try moving it to a slightly different spot.
- Check for Electrical Interference: If you suspect electrical interference, try moving the sensor away from any nearby appliances or devices.
- Contact Govee Support: If you suspect a sensor malfunction, reach out to Govee customer support for assistance. They can help diagnose the issue and provide guidance on potential solutions or replacements.

The Value of Accurate Leak Detection

While false alarms can be a nuisance, remember that the primary function of your Govee WiFi Water Sensor is to provide reliable leak detection and protect your home from potential water damage. By minimizing false alarms, you ensure that when a real leak occurs, the alert will be taken seriously and acted upon promptly.

By understanding the causes of false alarms and implementing preventive measures, you can maximize the accuracy and effectiveness of your Govee WiFi Water Sensor. This proactive approach ensures your system operates seamlessly, providing you with the peace of mind that comes with knowing your home is protected from the damaging effects of water leaks.

Chapter 6

Sensor Sensitivity Enhancement: Detecting Even the Smallest Leaks

Understanding Sensor Sensitivity

The Govee WiFi Water Sensor is a wonder of contemporary engineering: a little gadget that detects the presence of water and alerts you to possible leaks. But how can this little sensor accomplish such a feat? The answer is in its sensitivity, which affects its capacity to detect even the slightest amounts of moisture.

The Science of Sensitivity

Every Govee Water Sensor has a set of metal probes. When these probes come into touch with water, they conduct electricity and complete an electrical circuit. Water, being an excellent conductor of electrical, permits current to flow between the probes, indicating the presence of moisture. The sensor's sensitivity relates to its capacity to detect changes in electrical conductivity even in small volumes of water.

Why Sensitivity Matters

The sensitivity of a water sensor determines its efficacy. A very sensitive sensor can detect even minute amounts of water, such as a trickling drip or a little puddle growing under a sink. This early identification is critical in keeping small leaks from turning into large water damage problems. A less sensitive sensor, on the other hand, may only sound an alert when there is a sufficient volume of water present, enabling little leaks to go undetected and inflict severe damage over time.

Factors Affecting Sensitivity

The sensitivity of a water sensor may be influenced by many variables, including:

- Probe Material: The kind of metal utilized affects conductivity and sensor sensitivity. Govee Water Sensors make use of high-quality metals that have been specifically designed to detect water.
- Probe spacing affects sensitivity. Closer spacing often improves sensitivity, enabling the sensor to detect smaller quantities of water.
- The sensor's general design, including circuitry and components, might affect its sensitivity. Govee's sensors are precisely developed to assure peak performance.
- Environmental Factors: Temperature and humidity may impact sensor sensitivity. Extreme temperatures or high humidity may somewhat change the sensor's response.

The Value of Early Detection

Early identification of water leaks is crucial for reducing damage and avoiding expensive repairs. A very sensitive water sensor, such as the Govee WiFi Water Sensor, serves as an early warning system, alerting you to possible issues before they become severe. This enables you to take immediate action, such as cutting off the water supply or hiring a plumber, to limit the damage and avoid subsequent problems.

Beyond Leak Detection

While a water sensor's main role is to detect leaks, its sensitivity may be useful in other applications. For example, a sensitive sensor may be used to detect water accumulation in regions prone to condensation, such as basements or crawl spaces. This may assist to avoid mold development and other moisture-related issues.

Maintaining Sensitivity.
To guarantee that your Govee WiFi Water Sensor's sensitivity remains consistent over time, keep the probes clean and clear of debris. Regularly examine the sensors for evidence of corrosion or damage. If you encounter any problems, please contact Govee customer service for help.

Understanding sensor sensitivity and its usefulness in leak detection allows you to grasp the Govee WiFi Water Sensor's role in safeguarding your property. This insight allows you to make educated choices regarding sensor installation and maintenance, ensuring that your system functions with maximum accuracy and gives you the peace of mind you deserve.

Sanding Down the Sensor Feet: A Practical Guide

While the Govee WiFi Water Sensor is effective at detecting leaks, some users have found a creative way to increase its sensitivity and collect even the slightest quantities of moisture. This requires a modest change to the sensor's feet, enabling the water-detecting probes to make closer contact with the surface. Let's look at this practical technique for sanding down the sensor feet and improving your leak-detecting skills.

Understanding Sensor Sensitivity

The Govee Water Sensor has metal probes on the bottom that operate as main water detectors. When these probes come into touch with water, they complete a circuit, which activates the alarm and sends messages. However, the sensor's feet, which are meant to provide stability and avoid scratching, may sometimes leave a small space between the probes and the floor or surface where the sensor is positioned. This gap may, in certain situations, impair the sensor's capacity to detect trace levels of water or moisture.

The Benefits of Sanding

By gently sanding the sensor's feet, you may narrow the gap and bring the probes closer to the surface. This simple adjustment may dramatically improve the sensor's sensitivity, making it more sensitive to:

- Detect tiny leaks that may be missed.
- Detect thin water films, which may not activate the sensor in its original setup.
- Identify moisture buildup or condensation that may signal a leak or humidity issue.

Materials You'll Need

- Use fine-grit sandpaper (220 or above). This ensures a smooth finish and protects the sensor.
- Use a firm, flat surface, such as a workbench or table, for sanding.
- Optional: masking tape. If you want, you may use masking tape to shield the sensor's body from scratches when sanding.

Step-by-Step Sanding Guide

1. Prepare the sensor. Gently remove the sensor from its position and make sure it is dry. If desired, wrap masking tape over the sensor's body to prevent scratches.

2. Place fine-grit sandpaper on a level surface and fasten it to prevent movement while sanding.

3. Sand the Feet: Firmly hold the sensor and carefully massage the bottom of each foot on the sandpaper. Maintain uniform pressure and constant motion.

4. Monitor progress regularly. Periodically check the sanding process. You'll see the feet progressively becoming shorter. Stop sanding when the probes are almost flush with the bottoms of the feet.

5. Test the Sensor: After sanding, simulate a leak with a small quantity of water to ensure it works properly. Consider how fast and consistently the sensor triggers.

6. Clean the sensor. After testing, wipe off the sensor with a dry cloth to remove any sanding dust or debris.

7. Reinstall the sensor. Return the sensor to its proper placement, ensuring that it is firmly put on a level surface.

Important Considerations:

- Limit the amount of sanding on the feet. The idea is to decrease the space rather than eliminate the feet.
- Even Sanding: Sand each foot uniformly to preserve sensor stability.

- To protect the sensor, carefully remove any masking tape after sanding to eliminate residue.
- Test the sensor after sanding to ensure sensitivity and response.

Beyond Sanding

While sanding the feet may considerably improve sensitivity, keep in mind that other variables influence the sensor's effectiveness. Consider the following extra tips:

- \tOptimal placement: Choose leak-prone areas like sinks, appliances, and water heaters.
- Regular maintenance includes cleaning sensors and replacing batteries for maximum functioning.
- Regularly monitor the Govee Home app for sensor status updates and battery life indications.

By adopting a proactive approach to sensor sensitivity and following these practical suggestions, you can increase the efficacy of your Govee WiFi Water Sensor and guarantee it detects even the smallest symptoms of moisture, offering an extra layer of protection against possible water damage.

Testing Sensitivity After Modification

You've taken the proactive step of increasing the sensitivity of your Govee WiFi Water Sensor, allowing it to detect even the slightest leaks that might otherwise go unreported. Now it's time to put your changes to the test and ensure that your sensors are ready for peak performance.

This verification step is critical to ensuring that your leak detection system is ready to protect your house with absolute precision.

The Value of Post-Modification Testing

Consider this testing step to be a calibration for your newly upgraded sensors. It's a chance to check if the changes you made have boosted their sensitivity without having any unforeseen repercussions. Simulating a leak allows you to check the following:

- Improved Detection: Sensors now detect even tiny amounts of water or moisture and trigger an alert.
- Ensure reliable and constant sensor performance, even with minor water contact.
- Prevent false warnings from moisture or humidity by ensuring sensors are not excessively sensitive after adjustments.

Testing gives you assurance that your changes have produced the intended result: a highly sensitive leak detection system that can identify leaks early on, reducing possible harm.

Step-by-Step Test Guide

1. Prepare your testing area. Select a site where you can safely test the sensors without incurring water damage. A sink, bathtub, or small container will do wonderfully.

2. Gather your supplies. You will need a tiny quantity of water, a dropper or pipette for accurate water administration, and a dry cloth or paper towel to wipe up.

3. Test each sensor individually. Begin with one of the sensors you adjusted.

4. To simulate a little leak, use a dropper or pipette to delicately deposit a single drop of water on the sensor probes. Examine if the sensor causes an alert.

5. Gradually increase water volume: If the sensor does not respond to a single drop, add a few drops at a time until the alert sounds. Take note of the quantity of water necessary to set off the alarms.

6. Test Different Contact Points: Apply water to different places of the sensor's probes to confirm sensitivity across the sensing surface.

7. Repeat steps 3-6 for all modified sensors in the Govee WiFi Water Sensor 3 Pack.

8. Compare Sensitivity. Compare the sensitivity of original and changed sensors. This will allow you to assess the efficacy of your improvements.

Fine-tuning and Adjustments

According on your testing findings, you may need to make further changes to attain the required degree of sensitivity. If a sensor is insufficiently sensitive, examine the following.

- Re-sand probes. If you sanded the sensor's feet, you may need to sand them down even more to improve probe contact with the surface.
- Experiment with alternative placement locations to optimize contact with probable leak sources.

- Consider other techniques. If sanding does not offer the appropriate sensitivity, consider other methods, such as inserting a tiny, absorbent pad underneath the sensor to bring water nearer the probes.

Achieving the Right Balance

While more sensitivity is typically preferable, it is critical to find a balance. You want your sensors to detect even the slightest leaks, but not so sensitive that they cause false alarms due to condensation or humidity. If you discover that your customized sensors are prone to false alarms, try lowering their sensitivity by gently elevating the probes or using a less absorbent pad.

Confidence in Your Enhanced System

By properly testing your updated Govee WiFi Water Sensors, you can be certain that your leak detection system is performing optimally. This thorough approach guarantees that even the smallest leaks are spotted quickly, reducing possible damage and giving you precious piece of mind.

Chapter 7

Maintaining Your Govee Water Sensor: Ensuring Long-Term Performance

Battery Replacement: Frequency and Best Practices

Your Govee WiFi Water Sensors are powered by batteries, the unsung heroes that allow these devices to protect against any leaks. While the sensors are intended for energy economy and extended battery life, regular replacement is required to ensure their persistent monitoring. Let's look at some recommended practices for replacing batteries to keep your leak detection system running smoothly.

Battery life expectancy

Govee WiFi Water Sensors generally run for a long time on a single set of batteries. The actual lifetime might vary according to numerous variables, including:

- High-quality batteries last longer than generic or low-cost equivalents.
- Environmental Conditions: High temperatures and humidity might reduce battery performance and longevity.
- Frequent sensor activity, such as alerts or communication with the gateway, might use more power and cause quicker battery depletion.

While Govee sensors are built for efficiency, batteries should be replaced every 6 to 12 months. This proactive method guarantees that your sensors stay turned on and ready to detect leakage without interruption.

Choosing the Right Batteries

Govee WiFi Water Sensors commonly use AAA batteries. When looking for replacements, use high-quality alkaline batteries from respected companies. Alkaline batteries provide an excellent blend of performance, lifespan, and cost efficiency. Avoid using rechargeable batteries, since their voltage characteristics may be incompatible with the sensors, resulting in uneven performance.

Battery Replacement: A Step-by-Step Guide.

1. Gather your supplies. You'll need a fresh pair of AAA alkaline batteries and a tiny Phillips-head screwdriver.

2. Locate the Battery Compartment: The battery compartment is often located on the back or underneath the sensor.

3. Remove the Battery Cover: Using a Phillips-head screwdriver, gently loosen and remove the screws holding the battery cover.

4. Replace batteries: Remove old ones and install new ones, ensuring the polarity (+ and -) matches the indications within the battery compartment.

5. Secure the Battery Cover: Replace and tighten the screws tightly.

6. After replacing the batteries, verify the sensor by faking a leak to ensure it works properly.

7. Update the Govee Home App: Check the sensor's battery state. The app should show the updated battery level.

Proactive Battery Management

- Regularly check the battery status of your sensors in the Govee Home app. This enables you to locate sensors with low batteries and replace them quickly.
- Allow low Battery notifications: Check the app notification settings to allow low-battery notifications. This serves as a timely reminder to change batteries before they entirely drain.
- Keep extra batteries cool and dry, away from direct sunlight and severe temperatures. This helps to maintain their performance and lifespan.
- Environmental considerations: Properly dispose of outdated batteries by local legislation. To reduce their environmental effect, several shops offer battery recycling programs.

Beyond Battery Replacement.

While battery replacement is an important part of maintaining your Govee WiFi Water Sensors, frequent cleaning and inspections are also required. Keep the sensors clear of dust, dirt, and anything else that might interfere with their operation. By following these easy maintenance procedures, you can keep your leak detection system in excellent shape, giving you long-term safety and peace of mind.

Cleaning and Caring for Your Sensors

Your Govee WiFi Water Sensors are your vigilant protectors against water damage, standing guard 24/7 to alert you to potential leaks. To ensure these tireless sentinels remain in top form, a little TLC goes a long way. Regular cleaning and proper care not only extend the life of your sensors but also optimize their performance, guaranteeing they're always ready to detect and alert you to the first signs of trouble.

Why Cleaning Matters

Over time, dust, debris, and even mineral deposits from water can accumulate on your sensors, potentially interfering with their functionality. A buildup of grime can:

- Obscure the Probes: Dust or debris can coat the metal probes on the underside of the sensor, hindering their ability to detect water effectively.
- Impede Water Flow: Mineral deposits from hard water can form a crust on the probes, preventing water from making proper contact and triggering the alarm.
- Corrode Contacts: In extreme cases, prolonged exposure to dirt and moisture can lead to corrosion of the sensor's electrical contacts, affecting its performance.

Regular cleaning removes these obstacles, ensuring your sensors remain sensitive and responsive to even the smallest leaks.

Cleaning Your Govee Water Sensors: A Step-by-Step Guide

1. Power Down: Before cleaning, remove the batteries from the sensor to avoid accidentally triggering the alarm.

2. Gentle Wipe Down: Use a soft, slightly damp cloth to gently wipe down the exterior of the sensor, removing any dust or debris. Avoid using abrasive cleaners or harsh chemicals that could damage the sensor's casing.

3. Focus on the Probes: Pay close attention to the metal probes on the underside of the sensor. Use a cotton swab or a soft-bristled brush to gently remove any buildup or mineral deposits. If necessary, you can use a small amount of distilled water or isopropyl alcohol to help loosen stubborn grime.

4. Thorough Drying: Ensure the sensor is completely dry before re-inserting the batteries. Moisture trapped inside the sensor can affect its functionality or lead to corrosion.

5. Regular Cleaning Schedule: Aim to clean your sensors at least once every three months, or more frequently if they are placed in areas prone to dust or humidity.

Beyond Basic Cleaning

In addition to regular cleaning, a few extra care tips can help maintain the longevity and performance of your Govee Water Sensors:

- Avoid Extreme Temperatures: Do not expose the sensors to extreme heat or cold, as this can damage the internal components or affect battery life.
- Handle with Care: While the sensors are designed to be durable, avoid dropping them or subjecting them to excessive force, which could damage the casing or internal mechanisms.
- Keep Away from Chemicals: Avoid placing the sensors in direct contact with harsh chemicals, such as bleach or strong acids, which can corrode the sensor's materials.
- Store Properly: If you need to store your sensors for an extended period, remove the batteries and keep them in a cool, dry place.

Proactive Maintenance for Optimal Performance

- Cleaning and caring for your Govee WiFi Water Sensors is a small investment of time that pays off in the long run. By following these simple maintenance practices, you can:
- Extend Sensor Lifespan: Proper care helps prevent premature wear and tear, ensuring your sensors remain functional for years to come.
- Maximize Sensitivity: Clean sensors are more likely to detect even the smallest leaks, providing you with early warnings and minimizing potential damage.
- Reduce False Alarms: Keeping the sensors clean and dry helps prevent false alarms caused by dust, debris, or condensation.
- Ensure Peace of Mind: Knowing your sensors are well-maintained provides confidence that your leak detection system is always ready to protect your home.

By incorporating these cleaning and care practices into your routine, you can ensure your Govee WiFi Water Sensors remain reliable guardians against water damage, providing you with the peace of mind that comes with knowing your home is protected.

Chapter 8

Advanced Troubleshooting: Addressing Common Issues

Sensor Not Connecting? Troubleshooting Steps

Your Govee WiFi Water Sensors are your faithful partners in the fight against water damage, but like any technology, they may sometimes malfunction. One of the most typical difficulties that consumers have is a sensor failing to connect or losing connectivity to the gateway. While this might be irritating, it is often addressed with a few easy troubleshooting steps. Let us provide you with the expertise to identify and fix these connection issues, ensuring that your leak detection system stays attentive and trustworthy.

Understanding The Connection Process

Before we begin troubleshooting, it's important to understand how the Govee WiFi Water Sensor creates and maintains a connection. The system is based on two basic communication pathways:

1. Sensor to Gateway: The sensors connect wirelessly with the gateway via a low-power radio frequency. This link is critical for transferring leak detection notifications from the sensor to the gateway.

2. Gateway to WiFi Router: The gateway connects to your home WiFi network and sends warnings to your smartphone using the Govee Home app.

A disturbance in one of these channels might cause connection concerns. Let's look at the typical reasons and remedies.

Troubleshooting Sensor Connection Issues

If a sensor is not connecting or has lost its connection to the gateway, try the following troubleshooting steps:

1. Check battery life. The most prevalent cause of connection troubles is insufficient battery power. Replace the batteries with new, high-quality alkaline ones and check whether the sensor reconnects.

2. Verify Sensor Range: Ensure the sensor is within the suggested range of the gateway, usually approximately 100 feet in open spaces. Obstacles such as walls and floors may limit its range. If the sensor is too far away, consider placing it closer to the gateway.

3. Reduce Interference: Electronic equipment like microwaves, cordless phones, and baby monitors may interfere with the sensor's radio frequency. Try relocating the sensor away from any possible sources of interference.

4. Check for Obstructions: Make sure there are no physical barriers between the sensor and gateway, such as metal items or thick walls. These may disrupt or diminish the signal.

5. Re-pair the Sensor: If the connection between a sensor and the gateway becomes corrupted, try re-pairing it using the methods in Chapter 2 of this book.

6. Restart the gateway to repair connection difficulties. Unplug the gateway from the power outlet, wait a few seconds, and then reconnect it.

7. Ensure the sensor and gateway have the most recent firmware upgrades loaded. Outdated firmware may sometimes create connection issues.

8. Test with another sensor: whether you have numerous sensors, consider changing their places to see whether the fault is with the sensor or its placement. If another sensor operates in the same location, the first sensor might be malfunctioning.

Troubleshooting Gateway Connectivity Issues.

If the gateway cannot connect to your WiFi network or has lost its connection, take these steps:

1. Check WiFi Router: Make sure your WiFi router is working properly and your internet connection is active. Try rebooting your router.

2. Double-check WiFi Password: Enter the right password in the Govee Home app. Passwords are case-sensitive, so enter them exactly as they appear in your router settings.

3. Simplify WiFi Network Name (SSID) and Password: Some users have difficulty connecting to WiFi networks with complicated names or passwords that contain special characters. Try simplifying your network name and password to see if it fixes the problem.

4. Check WiFi Frequency: The Govee gateway normally uses the 2.4 GHz WiFi frequency. If your router broadcasts both 2.4 GHz and 5 GHz networks, make sure the gateway is on the 2.4 GHz network.

5. Reduce WiFi Congestion: To enhance the gateway's connectivity, temporarily unplug certain devices from the WiFi network.

6. Relocate the Gateway: Move the gateway closer to your WiFi network for better signal strength. Avoid putting the gateway near thick walls or metal items that might disrupt the signal.

7. Reset Gateway: If other troubleshooting methods fail, reset the gateway to factory default settings. This will delete all prior setups, so you will have to start from scratch.

Seeking Further Assistance

If you've tried every troubleshooting step and are still having connection problems, don't hesitate to contact Govee customer care. They offer a specialized staff of professionals who can give tailored help and advice. You may contact them via the Govee Home app, their website, or email.

Proactive Monitoring and Maintenance.
To reduce the chance of future connection difficulties, try following preventive actions.

- Regularly check the sensor battery life in the Govee Home app and replace it when low.

- Restart the gateway every few months to eliminate transient issues and maintain maximum performance.
- Regularly check for firmware upgrades for sensors and gateway to get bug fixes and performance improvements.

By understanding these troubleshooting procedures and doing preventative maintenance, you can guarantee that your Govee WiFi Water Sensor stays a dependable and watchful guardian against water damage, giving you the peace of mind that comes with knowing your house is secure.

App Not Updating? Solutions and Workarounds

While the Govee WiFi Water Sensor is intended to operate smoothly, rare hitches may occur, as with any technology. But do not be afraid! This chapter provides you with the information and resources you need to diagnose common difficulties and restore your leak detection system to peak performance, assuring your home's continuous safety.

Troubleshooting an unresponsive app.

If you notice that the Govee Home app isn't updating with the most recent sensor data or that messages aren't arriving as expected, here are some troubleshooting methods to get things back on track:

1. Refresh the App: Simple solutions are frequently the most effective. Swipe down from the app's main screen to refresh the data and force it to sync with the sensors.

2. Check your internet connection. Ensure that your smartphone or tablet has a reliable internet connection. To rule out connection difficulties on your device, turn off WiFi and then on again, or connect to another network.

3. Restart Govee Gateway. Unplug the gateway from the power outlet, wait a few seconds, then reconnect it. This often overcomes transient communication difficulties.

4. Verify sensor connectivity. Ensure that the sensors are within range of the gateway and have not been relocated or blocked. If a sensor seems offline in the app, try moving it closer to the gateway.

5. Check for app updates. An outdated app might sometimes create functioning concerns. Go to the App Store or Google Play to make sure you have the most recent version of the Govee Home app loaded.

6. Re-Pair Sensors: If a sensor is frequently unresponsive, consider deleting it from the app and re-pairing it with the gateway. This may reset the connection and repair communication issues.

7. Contact Govee Support. If the problem continues, do not hesitate to contact Govee customer service. They have access to more complex diagnostic tools and may provide tailored support.

Addressing Continuous Beeping

A sensor's continual beeping typically implies one of two things: a leak has been discovered or the sensor is malfunctioning. Here's how to detect and remedy the problem:

1. Check for water. First and foremost, check the area surrounding the beeping sensor for evidence of water. If a leak is discovered, it should be addressed immediately. When the water has been cleared, the sensor should cease beeping.

2. Inspect the sensor. If there is no leak, check the sensor for any obvious damage or debris that might be causing the warning. Clean the sensor carefully, giving particular attention to the probes.

3. Test the sensor: Simulate a leak by placing the sensor in a small amount of water. If it doesn't beep or continues beeping erratically, the sensor may be malfunctioning.

4. Replace the batteries. Low batteries can sometimes cause erratic behavior. Try replacing the batteries with fresh ones.

5. Contact Govee Support: If the beeping persists despite these efforts, contact Govee support for assistance. They can help determine if the sensor needs to be replaced.

Restoring Gateway Connectivity
The gateway is the central hub of your Govee WiFi Water Sensor system, so it's essential to keep it online. If the gateway appears offline in the app or you're experiencing connectivity issues, try these troubleshooting steps:

1. Check the Gateway's LED: The LED on the gateway provides visual cues about its status. A solid blue light indicates a successful WiFi connection, while a flashing blue light suggests it's trying to connect. Refer to the user manual for a complete guide to the LED indicators.

2. Verify Router Connection: Ensure the gateway is within range of your WiFi router and that the router is functioning correctly. Restart your router if necessary.

3. Check for WiFi Interference: Other devices or appliances emitting radio waves can sometimes interfere with the gateway's WiFi signal. Try moving the gateway away from potential sources of interference.

4. Simplify Your WiFi Network: Complex WiFi network configurations, such as those with mesh networks or advanced security settings, can sometimes cause connectivity issues. Try simplifying your network settings or using an older device with only 2.4 GHz WiFi for initial setup.

5. Reset the Gateway: As a last resort, you can reset the gateway to its factory settings. This will erase all previous configurations, so you'll need to set it up again from scratch. Refer to the user manual for instructions on how to reset the gateway.

Proactive Maintenance for Long-Term Performance
In addition to troubleshooting specific issues, proactive maintenance can go a long way in ensuring the long-term performance of your Govee WiFi Water Sensor system:

- Regularly Check Sensor Batteries: Replace batteries every 6-12 months to avoid unexpected disruptions in leak detection.
- Keep Sensors Clean: Clean the sensors every few months to remove dust, debris, and mineral deposits that can interfere with their functionality.
- Monitor the App: Periodically check the Govee Home app for any alerts or notifications, even if you haven't heard any alarms.
- Stay Updated: Keep the Govee Home app and your smartphone's operating system updated to benefit from the latest bug fixes and performance improvements.

By familiarizing yourself with these troubleshooting techniques and incorporating proactive maintenance into your routine, you can ensure your Govee WiFi Water Sensor system remains in peak condition, providing you with reliable leak detection and peace of mind for years to come.

Chapter 9

Govee Water Sensor vs. the Competition: A Comparative Analysis

Exploring Alternative Leak Detection Systems

The Govee WiFi Water Sensor offers a compelling combination of features and affordability, but it's not the only player in the smart leak detection arena. To make an informed decision about the best system for your needs, it's worth exploring alternative solutions and comparing their strengths and weaknesses. This chapter delves into the world of smart leak detectors, examining notable competitors to the Govee Water Sensor and providing a comprehensive overview of their capabilities.

1. Flo by Moen Smart Water Shutoff

Flo by Moen takes leak detection to the next level by integrating a smart water shutoff valve. This device not only detects leaks but can also automatically shut off your home's main water supply to prevent catastrophic damage. Here's a closer look at its features:

- Leak Detection and Prevention: Flo uses sensors to monitor water pressure, flow rate, and temperature, identifying leaks as small as a drop per minute. If a significant leak is detected, the system automatically shuts off the water supply.
- Remote Monitoring and Control: The Flo app provides real-time insights into your home's water usage, allowing you to monitor

water flow, set leak alerts, and even remotely shut off the water supply from anywhere in the world.

- Water Usage Analysis: Flo provides detailed reports on your water consumption habits, helping you identify potential areas for conservation and savings.
- Optional Installation: While professional installation is recommended, Flo offers a DIY option for those comfortable with basic plumbing.

Key Considerations:

- Higher Price Point: The Flo by Moen system is significantly more expensive than the Govee Water Sensor, primarily due to the inclusion of the smart water shutoff valve.
- Installation Complexity: While a DIY option is available, installing the shutoff valve may require some plumbing expertise.
- Subscription Service: Flo offers optional subscription plans that provide additional features, such as extended warranty coverage and advanced water usage analysis.

2. Phyn Smart Water Assistant

Phyn focuses on comprehensive water monitoring and leak detection, providing detailed insights into your home's plumbing system. Here's what sets it apart:

- Advanced Leak Detection: Phyn uses high-definition ultrasonic sensors to analyze the unique "fingerprint" of your home's water pressure waves, identifying leaks with exceptional accuracy.

- Water Usage Breakdown: The Phyn app provides a detailed breakdown of water usage by fixture, helping you pinpoint areas of high consumption and potential leaks.
- Automated Leak Response: Phyn can automatically shut off your home's water supply in the event of a catastrophic leak, preventing extensive damage.
- Pre-Freeze Warning: The system can detect conditions that may lead to frozen pipes, providing alerts to help you take preventive measures.

Key Considerations:

- Premium Price: Phyn is another premium-priced option, exceeding the cost of the Govee Water Sensor.
- Professional Installation: Phyn typically requires professional installation, adding to the overall cost.
- Data Dependence: Phyn's advanced leak detection relies on continuous data analysis, which may require a stable internet connection and could raise privacy concerns for some users.
- Honeywell Lyric Water Leak and Freeze Detector
- Honeywell offers a reliable and user-friendly leak detection solution with its Lyric Water Leak and Freeze Detector. Here are its key features:
- Wireless Sensors: The system uses wireless sensors that can be placed throughout your home to detect leaks and temperature changes.
- Audible and Visual Alerts: The sensors emit a loud alarm and flash a bright LED light when a leak is detected.
- Remote Notifications: The Honeywell Lyric app sends notifications to your smartphone, alerting you to leaks even when you're away from home.

- Optional Hub Integration: The sensors can be integrated with a Honeywell Lyric hub for enhanced functionality and control.

Key Considerations:

- Limited Sensor Range: The wireless sensors have a limited range, so you may need multiple hubs if you have a large home.
- Basic Functionality: Compared to Flo by Moen and Phyn, the Honeywell Lyric system offers more basic leak detection capabilities.
- Battery Dependence: The sensors rely on batteries, so you'll need to replace them periodically.
- Choosing the Right System for Your Needs
- When evaluating these alternatives alongside the Govee WiFi Water Sensor, consider your specific needs and priorities:
- Budget: The Govee Water Sensor offers a budget-friendly entry point into smart leak detection. If cost is a primary concern, Govee provides excellent value.
- Functionality: If you require advanced features like automatic water shutoff or detailed water usage analysis, Flo by Moen or Phyn may be worth the investment.
- Installation: Govee and Honeywell offer DIY-friendly installation, while Flo by Moen provides an optional DIY option. Phyn typically requires professional installation.
- Monitoring and Control: All systems offer remote monitoring and control through their respective apps. Consider the app's user interface and features when making your decision.

By carefully weighing these factors, you can choose the smart leak detection system that best aligns with your requirements and provides the level of protection and peace of mind you seek for your home.

Feature Comparison: Govee vs. Other Brands

You've made a wise decision to explore the world of smart leak detection with the Govee WiFi Water Sensor 3 Pack. But as with any technology purchase, it's always prudent to consider the alternatives and see how your chosen product stacks up against the competition. This chapter provides a comparative analysis of the Govee Water Sensor and other popular brands, empowering you to make an informed decision and reaffirm your confidence in your choice.

Key Features to Consider

When comparing smart leak detection systems, several key features warrant close attention:

- Sensor Sensitivity: The ability to detect even the smallest leaks is paramount. Look for sensors with responsive probes and adjustable sensitivity settings.
- Wireless Range: Ensure the sensors have a sufficient wireless range to cover the areas of your home where you need them most. Consider systems with a strong signal and minimal interference issues.
- App Functionality: A user-friendly app is crucial for monitoring your sensors, receiving alerts, and customizing settings. Look for apps with intuitive interfaces, clear notifications, and advanced features like automation and integration with other smart home devices.
- Alarm Loudness: The sensor's built-in alarm should be loud enough to alert you to a leak, even if you're in a different part of the house.

- Battery Life: Long battery life minimizes the hassle of frequent replacements. Look for systems with a battery life of at least six months to a year.
- Price: Compare the overall cost of the system, including the number of sensors, the gateway, and any subscription fees.
- Installation and Setup: Consider the ease of installation and setup. Look for systems with clear instructions and user-friendly pairing processes.
- Customer Support: Reliable customer support can be invaluable if you encounter any issues or have questions about the system.
- Govee vs. the Competition: A Head-to-Head Comparison
- To provide a comprehensive overview, let's compare the Govee WiFi Water Sensor 3 Pack to two other popular brands in the market: the Flo by Moen Smart Water Shutoff and the Ring

Alarm Flood & Freeze Sensor.

Feature	Govee WiFi Water Sensor 3 Pack	Flo by Moen Smart Water Shutoff	Ring Alarm Flood & Freeze Sensor

Sensor Sensitivity	Adjustable sensitivity through probe modification	High sensitivity with automatic leak detection	Moderate sensitivity
Wireless Range	Good range within a typical home	Excellent range throughout the entire home	Limited range, requires Ring Alarm Base Station
App Functionality	User-friendly app with basic monitoring and notification features	Feature-rich app with advanced monitoring, water usage analysis, and automatic shutoff capabilities	Integrated with the Ring Alarm system, offers security monitoring and automation features
Alarm Loudness	Loud built-in alarm	Loud alarm with optional push notifications	Relies on Ring Alarm siren and app notifications
Battery Life	Up to 1 year	Up to 2 years	Up to 3 years

Price	Budget-friendly option	Premium price point	Mid-range price, requires Ring Alarm system
Installation and Setup	Relatively easy setup with potential WiFi connectivity challenges	Professional installation recommended	Easy DIY installation, requires Ring Alarm Base Station
Customer Support	Responsive customer support with online resources	Excellent customer support with professional installation options	Comprehensive customer support with online and phone assistance
Additional Features	None	Automatic water shutoff, water usage monitoring, leak history, and potential insurance discounts	Integration with Ring Alarm security system, temperature monitoring, and optional professional monitoring

	Pros		
Pros	Affordable, easy to use, expandable with additional sensors	Comprehensive leak prevention and water management system with potential insurance savings	Seamless integration with Ring Alarm security system, long battery life
Cons	Potential WiFi connectivity issues, basic app functionality	High price point, professional installation recommended	Limited range, requires Ring Alarm system

Choosing the Right System for Your Needs

As you can see, each system has its own strengths and weaknesses. The Govee WiFi Water Sensor 3 Pack stands out as a budget-friendly option that's easy to use and provides reliable leak detection. It's an excellent choice for homeowners looking for a basic yet effective solution to protect their homes from water damage.

The Flo by Moen Smart Water Shutoff offers a more comprehensive approach with advanced features like automatic water shutoff and water usage monitoring. However, it comes at a premium price point and may require professional installation.

The Ring Alarm Flood & Freeze Sensor is a good option for those already invested in the Ring Alarm ecosystem. It offers seamless integration with the security system and provides additional features like temperature monitoring. However, it has a limited range and requires the Ring Alarm Base Station.

Ultimately, the best choice depends on your individual needs and budget. Consider the size of your home, the areas you want to monitor, and the level of functionality you desire.
By carefully evaluating the features, pros, and cons of each system, you can make an informed decision and choose the smart leak detection solution that's right for you.

Chapter 10

Conclusion: Enjoy Peace of Mind with Smart Leak Detection

Recap of Key Takeaways

As we reach the end of this comprehensive guide, it's time to reflect on the key takeaways and empower you to confidently embrace the world of smart leak detection with your Govee WiFi Water Sensor 3 Pack.

Embracing Proactive Protection
Throughout this guide, we've delved into the intricacies of the Govee Water Sensor, exploring its features, setup, troubleshooting, and maintenance. The overarching theme has been one of proactive protection – taking charge of your home's safety by implementing preventive measures against the costly and disruptive effects of water damage.

By investing in this smart home technology, you're not merely reacting to leaks after they occur; you're establishing a vigilant defense system that provides early warnings, minimizes damage, and grants you invaluable peace of mind.

Key Takeaways for Confident Leak Detection

Let's recap the essential knowledge you've gained on your journey to mastering the Govee WiFi Water Sensor:

- Understanding the System: You've become familiar with the components of the Govee Water Sensor, including the gateway, sensors, and the Govee Home app. You understand how these elements work together to create a comprehensive leak detection system.
- Mastering the Setup: You've learned how to set up the gateway, pair the sensors, and configure the app to suit your preferences. You're equipped to overcome potential WiFi challenges and ensure a smooth setup process.
- Strategic Placement: You now appreciate the importance of strategically placing the sensors in high-risk areas of your home, maximizing their ability to detect leaks early on.
- Sensitivity Enhancement: You've discovered techniques to enhance the sensitivity of your sensors, ensuring they can detect even the smallest leaks or moisture buildup.
- Effective Monitoring: You're skilled in using the Govee Home app to monitor sensor status, battery life, and receive timely alerts. You can customize notification settings and explore advanced features to personalize your experience.
- Troubleshooting and Maintenance: You're prepared to troubleshoot common issues, such as connectivity problems, false alarms, or sensor malfunctions. You understand the importance of regular cleaning and maintenance to ensure long-term performance.

The Govee Advantage

The Govee WiFi Water Sensor offers several advantages that make it a compelling choice for homeowners seeking reliable leak detection:

➤ Affordability: Compared to more complex or professionally installed systems, the Govee Water Sensor provides an accessible entry point into the world of smart leak detection.

➤ Ease of Use: Despite occasional setup challenges, the system is designed for user-friendliness, with an intuitive app and straightforward installation.

➤ Wireless Freedom: The wireless sensors can be placed virtually anywhere in your home, providing flexibility and convenience.

➤ Remote Monitoring: The Govee Home app allows you to monitor your home from anywhere with an internet connection, providing peace of mind even when you're away.

➤ Smart Home Integration: The Govee Water Sensor can integrate with other smart home devices, expanding its functionality and creating a more connected home environment.

➤ Beyond the Device: Cultivating a Leak Prevention Mindset

➤ While the Govee Water Sensor is a powerful tool in your leak prevention arsenal, it's essential to cultivate a proactive mindset and incorporate other preventive measures into your home maintenance routine:

➤ Regular Inspections: Periodically inspect your plumbing, appliances, and fixtures for any signs of wear and tear or potential leaks.

➤ Timely Repairs: Address any plumbing issues promptly to prevent them from escalating into major leaks.

➤ Seasonal Maintenance: Prepare your home for changing weather conditions by insulating pipes, sealing windows, and maintaining gutters to prevent water damage.

➤ Know Your Water Shut-Off Valve: Familiarize yourself with the location of your main water shut-off valve so you can quickly stop the water flow in case of a major leak.

By combining the Govee WiFi Water Sensor with these proactive practices, you create a comprehensive leak prevention strategy that safeguards your home and provides long-term peace of mind.